COLLEGE LONDON

GW00503300

Piano
Grade 6

Pieces & Exercises
for Trinity College London exams

2015-2017

Published by
Trinity College London
www.trinitycollege.com

Registered in England
Company no. 02683033
Charity no. 1014792

Printed in England by Caligraving Ltd.

The Fall of the Leafe

from *The Fitzwilliam Virginal Book*

Martin Peerson
(1571/3-1651)

All musical indications are editorial

Andantino Grazioso

Second movement from Sonata in F

Jan Ladislav Dussek
(1760-1812)

4

[Blank page to facilitate page turns]

Sonatina

op. 36 no. 6

Muzio Clementi
(1752–1832)

Allegro con spirito ♩ = 112

Prayer of the Matador

from *Lyric Pieces for the Young*

Norman Dello Joio
(1913–2008)

Valse lente

Oskar Merikanto
(1868–1924)

Evocation

from *Variations sur un Thème de Chopin*

Federico Mompou
(1893–1987)

Jazzin' Grace

Garry A F Wilkinson
(born 1958)

In a relaxed swing style ♩ = 94

The Wit and Wisdom of the Night

with a nod to Leonard Bernstein

Mark Tanner
(born 1963)

Castle Ward

Temple Dancer in Blue

June Armstrong
(born 1951)

Exercises

1a. Make it Fit! – tone, balance and voicing

1b. A Song – tone, balance and voicing

2a. Stubborn – co-ordination

Drammatico molto ritmico ♩ = 120

2b. Confused – co-ordination

Con moto ♩ = 92

3a. A Lucky Find – finger & wrist strength and flexibility

3b. Valse Triste – finger & wrist strength and flexibility

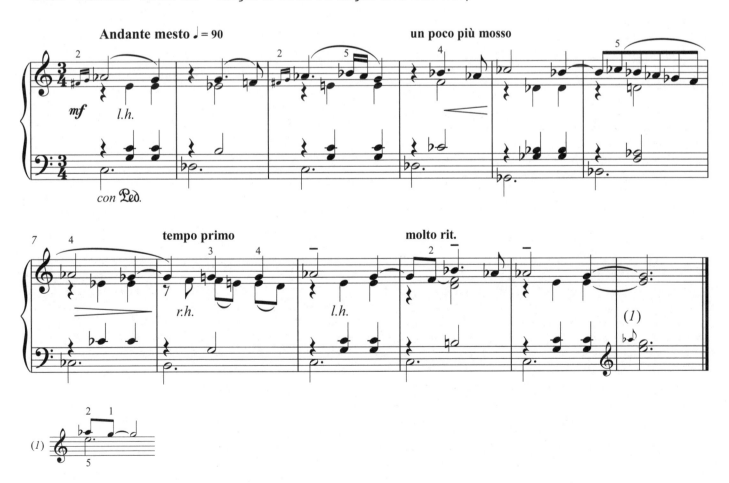

Teaching notes

Group A

Peerson   The Fall of the Leafe   page 2

The Fitzwilliam Virginal Book, from which this piece is taken, is an important compilation of nearly 300 Elizabethan/Jacobean pieces (musically, covering the late renaissance and very early baroque eras) named after Viscount Fitzwilliam, who bequeathed the collection to Cambridge University in 1816. Other composers, better known, include William Byrd and John Bull. Most pieces in it suit any keyboard of the time – not just the virginals but also harpsichord, spinet or even small organ. A quiet, intimate style is therefore required, particularly on the potentially over-powerful modern piano. Leaves fall at a melancholy time of year – autumn, when the days get shorter. The little sighing figures in bars 5-6 and their decorated versions in bars 13-14 should express this; the RH 'sighs' are obvious, but the slurred LH has them too. The tenor figure that ends every eight-bar section is a typical renaissance cadence decoration, and should be gently marked. Cadence chords themselves – and also the first three of the piece – may be discreetly arpeggiated. No pedal is necessary, anywhere. All ornaments should be quick, but without bumping.

Dussek   Andantino Grazioso (2nd movt from Sonata in F)   page 4

Born in Bohemia (now part of the Czech Republic), composition pupil of C P E Bach and resident in London for 10 years, Jan Ladislav Dussek was popular and influential in his lifetime but is today less well known than he might be. This extract from one of his 28 or so piano sonatas (there are more than 50 others, for violin or flute) is less showy and elaborate than much of his other music and recalls Mozart, also throwing a false recapitulation into the mix (bars 18-22) for fun. Its main melody should float expressively and calmly – its loudest dynamic is only *mf*. The correct tempo is critical: too slow, and it drags; too fast, and the decorations in, for example, bar 9 sound hectic rather than singable. The turn in bars 1, 18 and 27 may go as three before-the-beat grace-notes, as the printing implies – or as four equal demisemis, starting with (not before) the LH chord and incorporating the full-size quaver that follows. Other turns (bars 7, 9, 15 and so on) likewise incorporate the next full-size note, but go twice as fast, say, as four hemidemis. Count six in a bar: they start on the 'and' after '1' and reach the second semi – C in bars 7 and 9 – on the count of '2'. Keep a steady RH on the beat, LH after it, in bars 8 and 34, and avoid rushing through the suddenly slow notes of bar 10. The true recapitulation is regular, though notice that bar 32, at *mf*, reinforces the home key, unlike the equivalent bar 6, marked only *p* and modulating away from it.

Clementi   Sonatina, op. 36 no. 6,   page 7

More famous for his studies and teaching material, Clementi nevertheless wrote over a hundred full-scale sonatas or sonatinas, plus – among much else – four symphonies and a piano concerto. Beethoven was a great admirer: Mozart, on the other hand, warned his sister off playing his music, fearing that its technical demands might damage her natural technique! The op. 36 set has been popular with piano teachers ever since its composition. The idiom may be conventionally Mozartian, but the wide-ranging dynamics here – notice the many *ff*'s and *fz*s – invite more extrovert treatment. Some fingerings are crucial, like the RH thumb-markings in bars 20-21 making for an easy octave reach to the following high notes. Try practising bars like 30-31 in altered rhythms for secure co-ordination

of fingers, and to avoid uncontrolled rushing. Many *cresc./dim.* markings should confirm your natural instincts for phrasing. Other places, not marked, might include bars 40 and 42, effective with downbeat accents then *diminuendi*, and bars 48-51, where the harmony implies a slight accent on downbeats. The lack of a dynamic mark at the start tests your initiative: your choice, though the word *dolce* strongly suggests something less than *f*! Stay *f* until the marked *p* in bar 22; the *poco rall.* and pauses in bars 55-56 are compulsory, and a final bar *rall.*, though not marked, makes for an effective ending to a big piece.

Dello Joio   Prayer of the Matador   page 12

This sounds quite easy in performance, and its plaintive (American-composed but typically Spanish) melody sounds almost improvised. However, it needs careful shading between foreground and background, and the melody itself requires strict counting (in subdivided quavers) in order to emerge accurately. Bars 1-4 are no mere introduction but include an important tenor counter-melody in long notes: the up-and-down Es in the bass (in a *habañera* rhythm) should be much softer. Fortunately the piece is slow enough for you to calculate the right dynamic, note by note, bars 1-2 going *p*-(*pp*-*pp*-*pp*)/*mp*-(*pp*-*pp*)-*p*-*p* and so on, the *mp* not written but helping to shape the phrase. ('Accompaniment-only' bars 17-18 are, of course, all *pp* after the LH note.) Carefully distinguish between steady RH semiquavers, only two per quaver beat (bar 6), with fast triplet demisemis, those in bars 8 and 15 not starting until the 'and' after the count of '4'. Bar 12's (non-triplet) demisemis are slower, and should fill the first quaver beat without rushing. After a suddenly impassioned middle section (from bar 19) the opening melody resumes in bar 28, but without the *cresc.* to *mf* of equivalent bars 5-6. Bars 36-37 also die down sooner than equivalent bars 15-16: maybe our praying matador has lost heart, though not without a bit more passion from bar 39. RH takes the top three notes of bar 45's minim chord, carefully sustained with pedal as you add the final *habañera* touch in treble clef.

C P E Bach   Solfeggietto   *Faber*

In life, C P E Bach (J S Bach's second surviving son) was a calm and shrewd businessman. His music, however, sounds volatile and quite unpredictable. He wrote, among much else, 60 symphonies, countless sonatas, and a *Magnificat* that borrowed many ideas from the one by his father. The *Solfeggietto* is probably his best-known piece, and typically moody. The *f*'s and *p*s in bars 14-17 and 26-29 are all sudden: the *p*s could even be *pp*. Bar 24 is based on a diminished seventh, the most adventurous chord around at the time, and could even go *ff*; the following bar (with optional LH legato) is almost the only expressive moment in the whole piece. Most editions should clearly show which hand plays what in bars 1-12, 17-20 and from 31: stems down = LH, and stems up = RH, whatever stave they happen to fall on. Importantly, the swapping from one hand to another must be smooth and without bumps, the effect being of one hand playing everything. LH crotchets in bars like 13 and 15 may be pedalled: inauthentic, maybe, but adding colour and drama. Lift punctually for each crotchet rest. Bar 25's ornament may go as two grace-notes (D and Eb) starting on the beat rather than before it. For a dramatic and abrupt finish, play bar 35 with absolutely no *diminuendo*.

Britten	No. 1 from *5 Waltzes*	*Faber*

I doubt if anyone would guess the composer of this waltz without being told, but Britten was only 11 years old when he wrote it, something that could perhaps inspire would-be composer pupils of the same age. They would have to work hard to match the sheer quantity of music the young boy wrote: his diaries show that he began a new piece almost every day. This waltz is strictly classical in form (A–B–A) and idiom, the A sections in plain D minor and the 'B' section in B♭ (notice RH in bass clef here, from bar 25, where the printed fingering helps you bring out the top voice easily). Helpfully for slow learners, bars 42–51 are the same as bars 1–10. Watch for B♭s near C♯s in bars 11–12, and bring out interesting bass lines in bars 16 and 20–21. Continue pedalling as suggested in bars 1–2, though low-pitched bars like 11–12 and 15–16 might sound clearer without. The pauses closing each A section are compulsory – and make sure you end ***p***.

	Allegro moderato, 1st movt	
Diabelli	from Sonatina in B♭, op. 168	*Alfred*

Antonio Diabelli (1781–1858) was best known as a publisher of music by Beethoven, Schubert and Czerny, but wrote plenty of music himself. Beethoven wrote a gigantic set of variations on one of his waltz-tunes. This sonata-movement (**Moderato**, notice: 120 beats per minute is plenty) may remind you at times of Mozart and Haydn and needs similar performer skills, as do those composers: neat fingerwork (especially in the grace-note places, bars 18–19 and 62–63), reliable counting, controlled quiet LH (in bars like 9–11 and 18–21) shaping of expressive melodies, and an instinct for shading-off 'feminine-ending' cadences as in bar 8. The Alfred edition is particularly helpful for the last two requirements, (add RH *cresc./dim.*s around bar lines 8/9/10/11 and from 52/53) less so perhaps in pedalling: the printed suggestion in bars 9–11 (and in the recapitulation, bars 52–55) would muddy the RH rests. Try pedalling crotchet, nothing, minim in each bar – or none at all, if this is too awkward. The final long pedal (bars 68–72) may have sounded fine on Diabelli's own lighter-action piano, today too if RH was ascending not descending. As it is, RH will get drowned in reverberation unless pedal is changed more often. Experiment, and listen carefully. Pause frequently in bars 14–15 to check you are sustaining the right notes (and no others). Bar 31's bass A♮ disrupts a four-bar chromatic rise, and could conceivably be a misprint for A♭. Lift LH punctually in bars 5–7, 29–32, and particularly 42 as RH holds. The following **ritard.** is compulsory, for it signals the start of the recapitulation.

	Allegro burlesco, from	
Kuhlau	Sonatine in A minor, op. 88 no. 3	*Trinity*

Daniel Friedrich Rudolph Kuhlau's name – parts of it, anyway, if not all those Christian names – will be very familiar to piano teachers and middle-grade pupils. His life is less well known. German-born (1786) but later naturalised as Danish, he worked mostly in Copenhagen, as teacher and first flautist in the King of Denmark's orchestra. He composed a lot (as this piece's opus number suggests), but many of his manuscripts were destroyed in a house fire in 1832; the smoke from it brought on a chest ailment which killed him, tragically, the same year.

No tragedy here, as the word 'burlesco' (jokey) implies. This could have been called the 'Donkey' sonata, after all the hee-haws in bars like 8–10. The shorter ones elsewhere – right at the start, and every other place with a grace-note and octave jump – might even suggest the clucking of farmyard hens, a sound Haydn must have liked, for his own sonatas use it a lot. Technically, the piece needs controlled (not runaway) RH semiquavers, particularly during the long chromatic scales in bars 18–21 and 94–97. Be particularly rhythmic during these, or else you may lose your place and finish a note adrift. They dictate

your overall tempo, possibly not beyond 126 beats per minute. You need good scales elsewhere, and great broken chords from bar 55: practise this sequence in varied rhythms (pausing on, and/or accenting, the first notes of each group of four, then third instead, then fourth instead, then second; then the whole passage in dotted-semi-plus-demisemi pairs). There appear to be lots of notes to learn, but bars 77–112 are the same as 1–36. Any suggested finger-changes on the same note at the beginning work better for some players than others, and are not compulsory, but finishing the whole piece with a *rallentando* is a very good idea.

Group B

Merikanto	Valse lente	page 14

Oskar Merikanto is little known outside his native Finland, though his family was artistic: son Aarre was also a composer, and grandson Ukri a sculptor. On this evidence, Oskar favoured easy-going Romantic music, as did one of his Leipzig teachers, Carl Reinecke. This waltz's many changes of tempo must all be observed, though not exaggerated, or else the piece would simply sound unsteady. As the suggested metronome marks confirm, the **Andante** at bar 25 is slower than the previous tempo, and also slower than the very opening. The general *con Ped.* instruction invites experiment: try it mostly held in bars 1–4, lifting for the crotchet rests and changing on each new bass note from bar 3. There's more choice from bar 17: either respect the LH *staccatos* and pedal only second and third beats (or not!), or catch those *staccatos* in pedal to let them ring longer. Here, more certainly, bring out the lowest voice in RH, which is where the melody is hidden. LH slur plus *staccatos* from bar 29 invite a harp-imitation sound (*staccato* with pedal). Notice that hands are two octaves apart, unlike anywhere else, for bar 46's chord. If bars 49–50 are awkward at the (faster) speed you'd like, try re-arranging the hands so that LH takes the middle voice.

	Evocation (from *Variations*	
Mompou	*sur un Thème de Chopin*)	page 16

The subtitle should warn you what to expect, but the direct quotation from Chopin's Fantaisie-impromptu (bars 10–24) may still come as a surprise. This is no joke: Catalan composer Federico Mompou (who lived alternately in Barcelona and Paris) was no humourist but shy and retiring, often choosing to write music as simple as Satie. Big hands are helpful, though any out-of-reach tenths may be discreetly spread – always providing (as usual) that you catch the lowest note with pedal to avoid sustaining an incomplete chord. It often helps to start the spread on the beat rather than before it. The LH chord in bars 2 and 28 may be easier with its top note taken by RH. Learn the outer sections in *cantabile* single-bar units at first, but then connect them (despite the intervening rests) as well-shaped nine-bar phrases, swelling towards the discords in (you choose) bars 3 or 4 and not dying away too much before bar 9. The crotchet rests in bars 5 and 31 should instead be thought of as crotchet-tails, attached to and in unison with the bass F sharps, so as to preserve an unbroken tenor counter-melody.

Wilkinson	Jazzin' Grace	page 18

London-born trombonist, conductor, examiner and teacher Garry Wilkinson studied at Trinity College of Music, and his name may already be familiar as composer of a Grade 4 piece in the 2009-2011 syllabus. *Jazzin' Grace* is possibly the earliest of the new syllabus's jazz pieces: it starts gently, but the raucous bars 17–22 may remind grandparents (and archive film watchers) of 1950s rock pianist Jerry Lee Lewis – particularly if the long RH chords are rolled (tremolo'd) rather than just held, an option the composer originally sanctioned. Most players will already be familiar with the swung-quavers recipe shown at the beginning: this applies elsewhere too, possibly less obviously. Off-beat quavers, crotchets or dotted crotchets (see bars 2–4 for an example of each) all fall on the last third of the beat, not on its half. Grace notes may all be smeared: carefully articulating them would sound too 18th-century, definitely not what's wanted here. Bar 10 may be fingered either as written, or with RH 135 2-slide-2 1. Watch for flats continuing throughout the mysterious chords in bar 31. Pedal adds resonance and even a touch of percussion in the louder moments, but should definitely stay off through bars 33–34 for the final dissolve.

Tanner — The Wit and Wisdom of the Night — page 20

You'd be right to be reminded of *West Side Story* during this jazzy and catchy piece, from a collection entitled *Nightscapes*: its original subtitle read 'with a nod to Leonard Bernstein'. The opening $\frac{15}{8}$ time signature will amaze your friends, even those who think it means five dotted crotchets per bar. It doesn't always: as the bass-line and careful beaming of RH quavers tell you, this music switches between two- and three-quaver patterns (all equal length: no triplets), a device Bernstein may have borrowed from Bartók. The 'chutzpa' (or 'chutzpah') Mark Tanner asks for is a Yiddish word meaning extreme – almost cheeky – confidence. Draw dotted bar lines after the third bass-notes of bars 1 and 2 if you fear miscounting, and try re-fingering bar 2's RH crotchet-quaver-crotchet with 13-13-24 if necessary. The final Bs in RH of bars 4 and 6 are replayed (not tied) despite the slurs. Bar 10 is 'dry' (no pedal) but still starts *ff*. Leave room for 12 (unplayed) quavers while holding bar 11, holding bars 13 and 20 (with their pauses) even longer. Similarly, carefully count three quavers during one of the piece's few dotted crotchets (bars 18 and 19). Memorise RH from bar 14 (still in treble clef, notice) and look at LH to negotiate those leaps safely. Notice C♯s and F♯s throughout bar 18, and most of all, enjoy!

Armstrong — Castle Ward – Temple Dancer in Blue — page 22

This is the sixth of the *Strangford Sketches* by Belfast-based June Armstrong; Strangford Lough (together with the Ards Peninsula) being among her favourite places in Ireland. This piece's opening chords (and the cadence in bars 31–32) may remind you of Satie's famous *Gymnopédie no. 1*, but the principal melody is far more sophisticated, mixing Irish pipe-music with, as she puts it, 'a hint of swing'. In performance, this might imply delaying off-beat quavers a little (particularly as bars 56–58 are deliberately marked to be played 'straight'), though notice that bar 49 writes out accurately the amount of delay that normal jazz-playing would supply as a matter of course – so off-beat quavers notated in the normal way may need to swing a little less. In any event, first learn the melody strictly as written, observing the difference between quaver triplets and duplets, placing notes like the D in bar 8 strictly a semiquaver after the beat. When this is securely learned, then experiment with a touch of *rubato*, which may be more effective if set against a steady rather than erratic LH accompaniment. Notice F♮ against G♯ in bar 4, and F♮ in bar 23 after the previous bar's F♯. The very last spread chord implies an octave leap in LH 5th finger: if uncomfortable with this, consider taking A below middle C with RH instead, fingering the remaining three LH notes with 512 – caught and held, of course, with pedal.

J S Bach — Prelude in E, BWV 937 — Schott/Universal

This two-part-invention-like Prelude is not from the *48 Preludes and Fugues* but is no. 5 from the set of *6 Little Preludes* BWV 933–8, often published together with the *12 Little Preludes* numbered between BWV 924 and 999. Authentic editions offer no help with suggested dynamics or phrasing; older ones (recognisable as being full of slurs, dynamics, *crescendos* and so on) offer suggestions you can try out even if you subsequently discard them. Traditionally, in this kind of texture, semiquavers go *legato* and quavers detached, for contrast. This is not compulsory, though the four-note figure that starts bars like 2 (in RH) and 4 (in LH) is usually slurred. Emphasise the duet nature of the piece by playing the quaver tune louder (say *mf*) than the semiquavers (say *p*). Both hands could go *p* for bars 5–6, and could *cresc.* to *f* in bars 9–10. Bar 10's mordent ideally goes as two hemidemis plus one demi, starting on the beat, though two grace notes before the beat might be easier, and just one grace note may be passable for real strugglers. Bar 11 could start *p*, 12 could *cresc.* and 13 be *f* with accented tied notes. Check for E♯s through bar 14 (LH); try bringing out a melody hidden in bar 15–16's semiquavers (it goes crotchet, quaver rest, quaver, same again). Mark the LH four-note sequences from bar 17's F♯; bar 19's turn may be either a demisemi quintuplet starting on the D♯, or four demis starting on the E. Finish boldly (*f* and *poco rall.*), checking that top voice sustains over bar line 19/20.

Casella — Galop Final — *Boosey*

Early works by Turin-born Alfredo Casella (1883–1947) were ultra-romantic, and sound almost like Mahler. Later he became a neo-Classicist, writing music in modern idioms but recalling old-time musical forms. He may be best known today as an early editor of Vivaldi's *Gloria*. This *Galop*, however (French spelling, by the way), is quite the opposite, and sounds like silent film music. Practically anyone under 14 (and many people over) will love it. The faster the better (minimum probably ♩ = 152) – but bear in mind that it has to go even faster from bar 59 and faster still at 66. The suggested thumb-unders at bar 5 (and 8) add welcome accents, though any printed RH 2 and 4 in bar 20 is a misprint: its top-speed run-up should be fingered 2345 or 1234. Sustain bar 34's first chord during practice, to memorise its unusual sound. Bar 47 onwards is full of sharps, a comic modulation to a key (F♯ major) as far from the initial C major as is possible to be. Count carefully, especially if memorising: there are three bars of introduction (not four) to start with, and only one (not two) before bar 39. The cadence around bar line 66/67 comes three times, the one around bar line 69/70 four times. The very last chord needs careful reading, and memorising: each thumb plays two notes at once, and whereas LH spans an octave, RH spans a ninth. Keep the pedal down unchanged as you play it: the previous bass still applies.

Chopin — Cantabile in B♭, op posth (1034) — *Faber*

Although written (in Paris) well before Chopin's death, the *Cantabile* was not published until 1931: the manuscript is known through a 1925 photograph. At only 14 bars, it looks an easy exam option – but choose with care. It requires much subtlety, and instincts beyond just following the printed instructions. A well-shaped Romantic melody should taper off during bar 2 before building to bar 3; similar build-ups and taperings-off are needed in bars 9–10 and 11–12, while bar 12's RH B♭ needs sensitive matching to what remains of the previous long C. The basic tempo should perhaps be no more than ♪= 96: stretch this even more to close bar 3 without sounding hurried. Keep LH chords featherweight so as not to distract from RH melody, though bars 4, 8 and 10 may be brought out as secondary solos. Any printed pedal marks should over-ride *staccato* markings: each bass note must connect to the next. Bar 13's *smorzando* means 'dying away', and bar 14 should be held for the full six slow quavers.

The Little Shepherd
Debussy — (from Children's Corner) — *Trinity/Faber*

This dreamy and much-loved piece is rhapsodic but all the written rhythms should be observed without distortion: the quick theme but overall slow pulse may tempt you to miscount and move off too early, particularly in notorious spots like bars 6, 8-11, 14, 16, 20, 22 and 26. Count eight quavers per bar except just before triplets, which you should prepare by switching to a crotchet count then mentally subdividing one beat in advance: count bars 8 and 22 as 'one-and-two-three-and-a four-and-a'. At this speed, bar 23's three-against-two should be easy enough to work out mathematically.

Check for correctly lifted or sustained notes whenever one hand plays two parts, lifting LH E♯ in bar 8 when moving to F♯, lifting RH G♯ a bar later as you play F♯. Sustain RH F✕ to close bars 24-25 (yes, these come out as E♭ major chords). Much of the piece may go without pedal, but its use is compulsory through bars 10-11, 17-18 and (even quieter) 30-31 to sustain the written note values. Fight the inclination to re-pedal on the low bass fifths, but don't try to clear the very last minim rest, only possible with sophisticated trickery. Pedal also helps to fill the silences in bars 24-25 as hands leap from one position to another. Conversely, finger-hold bar 26's D♯ without pedal to leave it unaccompanied as other voices finish. Start the piece gently: bar 3 is more intense, bar 4 relaxed. Notice E♯ at the end of bar 20; check the new *cresc./dim.* in bar 21. Bar 25 is softer than 24, and bar 27 onwards is all softer than equivalent bars 5-11: adding *una corda* halfway through bar 29 may aid the closing ***ppp***. Most printed instructions affect the rhythm: **Cédez** means **rit.**, while the others are guessable.

Scherzando in A, from
Haydn — Sonata Hob XVI/36 2nd movt — *Peters*

Don't be confused by the key: Hob XVI/36 is a sonata in C♯ minor. This *Scherzando* is its middle movement, in a contrasted key, and mood, for the outer movements are mostly very serious. (The finale, believe it or not, contains a section in the rare key of C♯ major, all seven sharps of it!) It's a long movement, even without repeats (not played in the exam): the form is a kind of varied rondo, with a main theme in two parts (in A major then minor), each part being itself in two parts. Bars 34/35-64 are a variant of bars 0/1-30; bars 68/69-84 vary just bars 0/1-16. Short *ritornelli* start at bars 30/31, 64/65 and 84/85: the coda begins in bar 88 (best played *f*, and notice the scales a tenth, not an octave apart, in bars 90-91).

Printed repeat marks and key signature changes may tempt you to stop and start (e.g. in bars 16, 30 and 50), but it's vital to keep going in strict time with no pauses. Authentic editions may contain few dynamics: those that exist may help you decide what to do elsewhere. Bar 30/31 is marked ***p***: the identical theme at bar 0/1 and 64/65 could be the same. Bar 8/9 matches 42/43 (also marked ***p***); bar 82 (***f***) is a variant of bar 14 (therefore also ***f***). Unison in bars 22/23-26 implies ***f*** (*meno* ***f*** then *cresc.* from 26); bar 16 could therefore have gone ***p*** to make a contrast. Your edition may print bars like 1, 9 and 68/69 with appoggiatura, quaver and two semis: play four equal semis each time, starting on (not before) the beat. Bring out Haydn's child-like (not childish) humour with *staccato* quavers when repeated (bar 1 in both hands; bars 4-7 and later in LH), contrasting them with smooth harmony in bar 3. The RH turn in bar 18 can go as four demisemis, starting on a chord of A and D, then C, B and C. Probably no pedal, until the two last chords.

Teaching notes written by Michael Round

Key

A solid line denotes a piece within this book.

A dotted line denotes a piece from the alternative list.